14.95

SHARKS SET II

COMMON SAWSHARKS

Adam G. Klein
ABDO Publishing Company

visit us at
www.abdopub.com

Published by ABDO Publishing Company, 4940 Viking Drive, Edina, Minnesota 55435.
Copyright © 2006 by Abdo Consulting Group, Inc. International copyrights reserved in all
countries. No part of this book may be reproduced in any form without written permission from
the publisher. The Checkerboard Library™ is a trademark and logo of ABDO Publishing
Company.

Printed in the United States.

Cover Photo: © Marty Snyderman / SeaPics.com
Interior Photos: Corbis p. 19; © Doug Perrine / SeaPics.com p. 18; © Kike Calvo / V&W /
    SeaPics.com p. 10; marinethemes.com/Kelvin Aitken pp. 11, 13; © Marty Snyderman /
    SeaPics.com p. 17; Mike Parry / Minden Pictures p. 15; Peter Arnold p. 9; © Richard
    Herrmann / SeaPics.com p. 16; © Rudie Kuiter / SeaPics.com p. 21; © Saul Gonor /
    SeaPics.com p. 5; Uko Gorter pp. 6-7

Series Coordinator: Heidi M. Dahmes
Editors: Heidi M. Dahmes, Megan Murphy
Art Direction: Neil Klinepier

Library of Congress Cataloging-in-Publication Data

Klein, Adam G., 1976-
    Common sawsharks / Adam G. Klein.
       p. cm. -- (Sharks. Set II)
    Includes index.
    ISBN 1-59679-286-8
     1. Saw sharks--Juvenile literature. I. Title.

QL638.95.P7K58 2005
597.3--dc22
                                                                    2005050116

CONTENTS

COMMON SAWSHARKS AND FAMILY ... 4

WHAT THEY LOOK LIKE 6

WHERE THEY LIVE 8

FOOD 10

SENSES 12

BABIES 14

ATTACK AND DEFENSE 16

ATTACKS ON HUMANS 18

COMMON SAWSHARK FACTS 20

GLOSSARY 22

WEB SITES 23

INDEX 24

COMMON SAWSHARKS AND FAMILY

In the animal world, life is all about survival. Creatures use their instincts and abilities to meet every challenge. Even the most unusual creatures thrive when they use their natural gifts.

There are more than 200 living shark species. Sharks can see, hear, smell, taste, and feel. They are made of **cartilage** rather than bone. They have fins and five to seven pairs of gill slits. And, their skin is covered in **dermal denticles**.

Common sawsharks, also known as longnose sawsharks, are unusual creatures. They are easily recognized by their long, bladelike snout. This feature can seem strange and awkward. Still, sawsharks are fascinating and special animals.

Sharks normally spend their time alone. But, sawsharks are known to form schools.

What They Look Like

The common sawshark's flattened, bladelike snout is its most distinct feature. Long barbels hang from the underside of the saw. And, the snout is studded with both long and short teeth. The teeth are replaced when they are broken or lost.

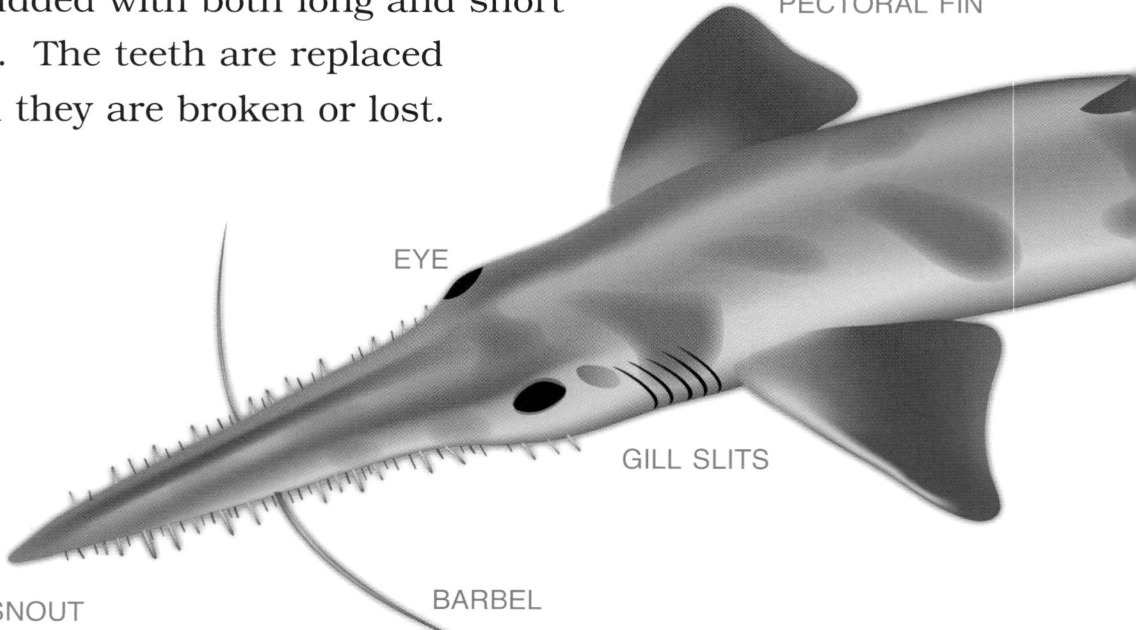

PECTORAL FIN

EYE

GILL SLITS

SNOUT

BARBEL

Sawsharks have flat, slender bodies. Males grow to 48 inches (122 cm) long. Like many shark species, female sawsharks are longer. The females reach lengths of 59 inches (150 cm).

The common sawshark has two **dorsal** fins. And, it has five gill slits on each side of its head. It has a small mouth that rests behind its enormous snout. The sawshark's back is covered with dark spots and blotches. The belly is a beige or yellowish color.

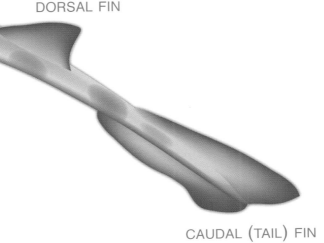

DORSAL FIN

DORSAL FIN

PELVIC FIN

CAUDAL (TAIL) FIN

Where They Live

The common sawshark is a **temperate** and subtropical Australian species. It lives in the eastern Indian Ocean along the Australian coasts and Tasmania. The common sawshark is found along **continental shelves**.

Common sawsharks are shallow-water creatures. Their bodies are adapted to living near the bottom of the ocean. Their flat form allows them to get close to the ground.

Sawsharks choose sandy areas to live in. During the day, they remain motionless on the seafloor. At night, they venture out to hunt. They dig through the sand, algae, and seaweeds to find their food.

The waters surrounding Australia contain about 70 shark species. Many animal species can only be found in this diverse part of the world.

FOOD

Sawsharks eat many different types of creatures. They feed on squid and small fish such as gapers and cornetfish. They also find **crustaceans** that are traveling on the ground. These creatures become tasty snacks for sawsharks.

A common sawshark uses its barbels as feelers to detect prey hidden in the sand. The sawshark swipes back and forth with its snout to dig up the creature. Then, the sawshark disables its prey by hitting it with sideways swipes.

Cornetfish are long and thin. Common sawsharks love to eat some species of cornetfish!

The common sawshark trails its barbels
along the seafloor to find its prey.

SENSES

Sharks have the same five main senses that humans have. But, they also have special senses that are adapted for their **environment**. For example, sharks detect pressure changes in the water. This allows them to determine water depth and which way is up.

Sharks also have special sensors called ampullae of Lorenzini. These sensors are actually **pores** that are located on the snout and lower jaw. Sharks use their ampullae of Lorenzini to detect electrical currents given off by living creatures.

Humans don't have a lateral line sense system either. Along each side of a shark's body are two sensory tubes that are the lateral line. The lateral line picks up vibrations in the water. These vibrations, as well as the electrical currents, will lead a shark to its next meal.

With their many senses, sawsharks can search out prey and avoid **predators**. Without the extra help, they would have difficulty surviving in the dark ocean.

A shark's sense of smell is important to its survival. In fact, sharks have been called "swimming noses."

BABIES

Developing sharks grow inside of the mother common sawshark. The babies are contained and protected in egg sacs. As they mature, the unborn sharks live off of nutrition in the eggs.

It takes about 18 months for the unborn sharks to develop. So, they are well developed when they are born and ready to survive on their own. Baby sharks are called pups.

Mother common sawsharks give birth to between 3 and 22 young. The pups are about 15 inches (38 cm) long at birth. Unlike many sharks, sawsharks are born headfirst.

The pup is born with the larger set of teeth on its snout. The teeth are soft and lay flat during birth. The blades eventually straighten and harden. And, smaller blades fill in between the larger ones.

Soon after they are born, the pups are on their own. The mother shows no awareness of her babies and swims away.

A common sawshark embryo. An embryo is an organism in the early stages of development.

ATTACK AND DEFENSE

Most sharks are **carnivores**. And, they eat live prey. But in addition to being hunters, many sharks are hunted for their meat. Many people find the meat to be a **delicacy**. The shark's skin is made into leather,

Different shark species are often hunted for their fins. This is harmful to shark populations because sharks are slow to reproduce.

and the teeth are sold as souvenirs.

A shark's best defense against **predators** is to hide. This is especially true for small or young sharks. The pups survive by remaining in nursery areas. Here, they feed on prey suited to their size. And, their skin coloring keeps them hidden.

The common sawshark's bladelike snout is its best defensive tool. If caught in a net, this shark can seriously harm a human attempting to free it. And with a few sideways swipes, the teeth on the snout can disable a creature.

The common sawshark's snout alone makes up 27 to 29 percent of its length.

ATTACKS ON HUMANS

Each year, there are about 100 shark attacks. Of these, about 25 percent are fatal.

Common sawsharks present little danger to humans. Sawsharks are not known to kill people. Sharks are only interested in finding meals that they are familiar with. They do not naturally prey on humans.

Sharks attack humans when they are bothered, hungry, or defending their territory. When people swim, their movements resemble those of a wounded animal. This could attract a hungry shark.

18

There are many ways to avoid being attacked by a shark. These include heeding shark warnings at beaches and avoiding swimming alone. You should not swim at dawn, at dusk, or at night. Sharks are most active at these times.

This diver is wearing a chain mail suit that will protect against this shark's bite.

COMMON SAWSHARK FACTS

Scientific Name:

Common sawshark   *Pristiophorus cirratus*

Average Size:

Males grow to 48 inches (122 cm) long.
Females are slightly larger. They grow to lengths of
59 inches (150 cm).

Where They're Found:

The common sawshark occupies the eastern Indian
Ocean along the Australian and Tasmanian coasts.

Common sawsharks can live to be about 15 years old.

GLOSSARY

carnivore - an animal or plant that eats meat.

cartilage (KAHR-tuh-lihj) - the soft, elastic connective tissue in the skeleton. A person's nose and ears are made of cartilage.

continental shelf - a shallow, underwater plain that borders a continent and ends with a steep slope to the ocean floor.

crustacean (kruhs-TAY-shuhn) - any of a group of animals with hard shells that live mostly in water. Crabs, lobsters, and shrimps are all crustaceans.

delicacy - a rare or luxurious food.

dermal denticle - a small toothlike projection on a shark's skin.

dorsal - located near or on the back, especially of an animal.

environment - all the surroundings that affect the growth and well-being of a living thing.

pore - a small opening in an animal or plant through which matter passes.

predator - an animal that kills and eats other animals.

temperate - having neither very hot nor very cold weather.

WEB SITES

To learn more about common sawsharks, visit ABDO Publishing Company on the World Wide Web at **www.abdopub.com**. Web sites about common sawsharks are featured on our Book Links page. These links are routinely monitored and updated to provide the most current information available.

INDEX

A

ampullae of Lorenzini
   12
attacks 18, 19

B

barbels 6, 10
belly 7
body 7, 8, 12

C

cartilage 4
color 7, 17

D

defense 13, 16, 17,
   18
dermal denticles 4

E

eggs 14
environment 8, 12,
   13

F

fins 4, 7
food 8, 10, 12, 13,
   14, 16, 17, 18

G

gills 4, 7

H

head 7
hunting 8, 10, 13, 16

I

Indian Ocean 8

J

jaws 12

L

lateral line 12

M

mouth 7

P

predators 13, 16
pups 14, 15, 16, 17

S

senses 4, 12, 13
shark species 4, 7, 8
size 7, 14, 16, 17
skin 4, 16, 17
snout 5, 6, 7, 10, 12,
   14, 17

T

teeth 6, 14, 16, 17

DATE DUE